Panoramas of the Far East

Panoramas of the Far East

Photographs by Lois Conner

Smithsonian Institution Press, Washington and London

Published in association with Constance Sullivan Editions

This series was developed and produced for the Smithsonian Institution Press
by Constance Sullivan Editions

Series editor:
Constance Sullivan

Smithsonian editor:
Amy Pastan

Designed by Katy Homans

The paper used in this publication meets the minimum requirements of the
American National Standard for Permanence of Paper for Printed Library Materials
Z39.48-1984

First edition

Printed by Meridian Printing, East Greenwich, RI, USA
Duotone separations by Thomas Palmer

Cover: Yangshuo, Guangxi, China, 1991

Xi Hu, Hangzhou, Zhejiang, China, 1984

When did you begin photographing in the Far East?

In 1984 I received a grant from the Guggenheim Foundation to photograph in China for eight months.

What attracted you to that particular place?

I became interested in photographing in China because of an art history class in Chinese landscape painting that I took at Yale. The hanging scroll and the hand scroll, used by Chinese painters for millennia, seemed like an ideal form for landscape with its exaggerated rectangle that extends the narrative. Studying the paintings made me wonder if there was something about the land that had inspired them to use this form.

    And at about the same time, I discovered that three different banquet cameras, 7 x 17, 8 x 20, and 12 x 20, were made in America until just after the turn of the century, and used primarily to photograph groups of people at banquets. So I cut out each of the shapes, put them together, and decided which one I liked best.

Did Chinese landscape painting influence your desire to work with the banquet camera?

Looking at these paintings made me think about the form of the photographs I was making. When I took the Chinese landscape painting class I was using an 8 x 10 view camera. Within a year I began using the banquet camera. But it was a lot more difficult to use than I had imagined because a very elongated, exaggerated rectangle makes it difficult to put things together in the frame. At first I tended to make everything radiate off the center rather than having a sweeping narrative, but the process became more fluid as I got used to the camera.

Why do you work with such a cumbersome instrument considering that you travel to remote, sometimes primitive, areas?

I work with this camera because of the way it describes the world. It can most accurately articulate what I see. I don't find it cumbersome because I worked up to the 7 x 17 camera from 5 x 7 and 8 x 10 view cameras. Before my first trip to China, I traveled around Europe and the United States with the 7 x 17 and 8 x 10 cameras, which seems crazy in retrospect, but at the time I didn't think it was such a big deal. Of course, it's easier in Europe and America because you can hail a cab if you need one. In China I could handle only one camera because I was there for eight months and also had to carry 150 pounds of film, film holders, and a change of clothes.

Are your photographic trips to China well planned?

The first time I traveled in China, I made a general tour of major cities like Guangzhou, Shanghai, Beijing, Chengdu, and Guilin, and the surrounding areas, which gave me a sense of the vastness of the country. But I found it impossible to work with such a specific itinerary, so the following five months of that trip and on subsequent trips I made a loose itinerary that allowed for impromptu changes. I like to revisit places, even during the same trip, especially if I'm traveling for an extended period of time and the seasons change perceptibly.

I have a little tour that I take with my bicycle, or on foot. I go out all day with my camera to places that I've become attached to, and maybe I'll visit them five or six times before the photograph actually happens. Or one day it might be pouring rain and everything comes together. It's hard to describe what makes me stop and photograph a place, but I am attracted to certain places and the need to explore further that comes later when the weather conditions change or the light changes or maybe it's just the wrong season—when it's very leafy and full in the summer time, it's impossible to see the structure of the ground and of the trees.

When you rephotograph a particular place over a period of years, does your work change as a result of repeated visits?

The reason I'm attracted to a place changes with each visit and is reinformed by what I've seen in the interim. The work changes as my idea of what is photographic changes. For example, the photograph on page 47 was made during my third trip to China. I was fascinated the first time I saw this huge tree that had been felled by lightening laying in the middle of the courtyard. This image resulted from repeated visits.

People appear in many of your recent photographs, usually as part of the landscape, but sometimes you seem more concerned with them than their environment.

I'm interested in photographing people as being part of the environment, and am also intrigued with a more formal kind of portraiture.

Do you shoot a lot and edit extensively?

My work is heavily edited. Sometimes it takes me years to figure out that a photograph I made is actually not bad.

Do you print your work immediately after you develop the film?

I develop my film immediately. I've never had a chance to proof every photograph. Some of the pictures in this book were printed recently for the first time. I've found the passage of time to be one of the best editors because it separates me from the event or place and makes it easier to be objective.

What can you do with the panoramic camera that you might not be able to do with an 8 x 10 view camera?

Include more and extend the narrative. Chinese scroll paintings are meant to be read. Rather than taking in the whole painting, you observe a small portion and move along, seeing the landscape change as in a journey. Because it's not possible to take in the entire panoramic photograph in a glance (except at a distance), I think it invites a different kind of reading—perhaps similar to the scroll.

You've worked extensively in New York City and throughout the United States.

I started photographing in New York City parks in 1978. Three years later I found a new domain to explore, on another level—the roof. Although roof access is difficult, it's often surprising and always envigorating.

Since 1982 I have made biannual trips across country in my truck, lately spending more time in the Southwest.

Do you see differently when you're photographing New York City from a rooftop than when you're photographing a landscape in China or the Southwest?

I see it all as landscape that I'm curious to explore. I feel privileged to be able to go to these different places and observe a particular event, and want somehow to be able to describe that experience in a two-dimensional photograph.

What particular challenges do you have to deal with when photographing in the Far East?

Photographically, the challenges are similar to those of working elsewhere in the world. But cultural adjustments can be difficult. The rhythm is slower, so patience is essential for everything from buying train tickets to ordering a meal.

How do you transport yourself and your equipment?

Mostly local transportation, including trains, buses, boats, camels, oxen carts, and horses, to get to and from a general area. My daily transportation is by bicycle or on foot. I decided that I could easily balance a camera, film holders, and tripod on the back of my bicycle when I saw other people carrying a chest of drawers, two children, and a live pig on theirs.

Are there limitations regarding where you can go and what you can photograph in China?

Certain places in China are prohibited to foreigners because of the level of poverty or their proximity to a military installation.

Why is the platinum printing process important to your work?

In 1974 I started using a 5 x 7 camera and was amazed at how much information I could get onto the negative. But when I tried to print these negatives on silver paper, I found that the subtle information was missing in the print. The platinum printing process offers a fuller articulation of the tonal scale. It creates a sense of three-dimensionality and enables me to better describe such elements as volume, air, and weather.

You sometimes combine two or more frames to create multi-paneled pictures. Do diptychs and triptychs more successfully describe what you see than a single frame?

It's just a different vehicle for articulating what I see. There is nothing like the single frame, but I also love the possibility of putting many frames together, vertically and horizontally, because sometimes one frame doesn't accommodate what I saw as the photograph.

Are you interested in cultural and political events or are your photographs primarily concerned with aesthetic issues?

During the nine years that I've been photographing in China major changes have occurred on many levels. I'm aware and observant, but I am not a photojournalist. The quieter events and subtle changes are what I hope to capture in my photographs. Right now, the landscape is changing dramatically because of increased building construction, even in the smallest areas.

How do you decide what to photograph?

Deciding what to photograph is always a dilemma. But I don't think about it when I'm working, I just look and respond visually.

Do you usually know where you want to stand in relationship to what you are photographing?

Not really; but sometimes it is immediately apparent, as in the photograph of the ladder leaning against a tree. When I saw that ladder and the trees bathed in hazy morning light, I stopped and set down my camera, and by the time I actually made my exposure about three hundred people had gathered behind me. I recall trying to persuade them not to walk in front of the camera during the exposure. Although I was out all day, that's the only picture I took.

Is that frustrating?

No. I feel privileged to be out there all day exploring, and the time is never wasted because what I see and experience informs my work later. Sure, the film gets heavy and maybe I wish I had taken fewer film holders. But who knows what I might see at the end of the day or five minutes down the road?

Are landscapes, cities, architecture, and people all equally interesting to photograph?

I see them all as equal. My landscape photographs are like a portrait of the land, and that land is different wherever you go because the people who live there shape it by building specific structures or growing certain vegetation on it. Right now the two places that I find most exciting are Asia and the Navajo reservations in the American West.

I want to keep going back to the Four Corners area because I have a real affinity for the people and the landscape. I'm moved by both, but I'm not interested in one without the other. I recently began working on a project to photograph native Americans, starting with the Navajo reservation.

Chengdu, Szechuan, China, 1986

Yangschuo, Guangxi, China, 1985

Gaotien, Guangxi, China, 1991

Wanchai, Hong Kong, 1985

Chengdu, Szechuan, China, 1986

Shanghai, Jiangsu, China, 1984

Beijing, China, 1988

Wanchai, Hong Kong, 1986-1991

Zhouqing, Guangdong, China, 1985

Pagan, Burma, 1985

Dunhuang, Gansu, 1991

Turfan, Xinjiang, China, 1991

Kashgar, Xinjiang, China, 1991

Aishan, Guangxi, China, 1991

Yangschuo, Guangxi, China, 1991

Kathmandu, Nepal, 1985

Gaotien, Guangxi, China, 1984

Da Fu, Le Shan, Szechuan, China, 1986

Jomson trail, Nepal, 1985

Miyajima, Japan, 1991

Mandalay, Burma, 1985

Qing Nao, Guangxi, China, 1986

Kashgar, Xinjiang, China, 1991

Kashgar, Xinjiang, China, 1991

Hai Geng Yuan, Kunming, China, 1984

Yangshuo, China, 1991

Yangshuo, China, 1991

Irrawaddy River, Burma, 1985

Nara, Japan, 1991

Lois Conner

In their slim dimensions, pale layers of washy gray, and sense of perfect balance and repose, Lois Conner's photographs stand out from the efforts of her contemporaries. From her antique cameras to her technique of platinum-palladium printing, she is one of the most staunchly out-of-step artists at work today. Her panoramic landscapes have frequently been compared to Chinese scroll paintings; both view humankind with fragile tones, as a marked but ultimately minor presence. But what the master calligrapher achieves with the spontaneous strokes of a brush, Conner seeks through the deep focus of her lens.

Hers is a long look, whether at the slow workings of the countryside in Guilin, China, or across the rooftops of Brooklyn to the skyline of Manhattan. It is often a timeless, even an impersonal look. In her viewfinder, the many pieces of her landscapes are locked in a Renaissance grid. But within each imposed rectangle, the elements of her pictures—wooden watertowers, a ladder against a tree, the bamboo poles of an arbor built beside a river—swim against one another in a cold and refreshing harmony. Nothing seems extraneous in the thought-out, tautly constructed world that she sees.

Born on Long Island in 1951, Conner grew up in Delaware and Pennsylvania, two areas where she has photographed over many years. Her father, an electrical engineer who designs optical instruments and makes furniture, introduced her to photography at the age of nine. As a teenager she learned to develop film, print negatives, design jewelry, and make her own clothes—activities which seem to have determined her independent path. At the University of Delaware she studied painting and art history, and took her first serious courses in photography, but left before graduating. In 1971, she ventured to New York where she attended the Fashion Institute of Technology for two years and worked at the United Nations in a variety of jobs, including freelance architectural photographer.

Having decided to pursue a degree in photography, she entered Pratt Institute in 1973 and the following year took her first class in the operation of a view camera. "Once I used one, it seemed right. I bought one the next week," she says. At the same time she had begun to investigate platinum printing and in 1975 was awarded a Pratt Institute Research Grant, with her teacher, to study the process. She relied during those years on Deardorff 4 x 5 and 5 x 7 cameras, concentrating on landscapes and portraiture.

She photographed a housing project in Africa in 1976 for the United Nations Development Corporation, on the first of what became a pattern of excursions outside the country. In 1982, her father pieced together and presented her with a "banquet camera," so-called because its elongated format is ideal for including the several tables who would gather for such an occasion. During her first trip to China in 1984 (she has since returned on four more visits), she photographed extensively with this camera, which soon became her favorite. Conner carries her own equipment when she travels, a load which—with camera, tripod, and film holders—can amount to forty-five pounds or more. She also carries about seventy-five pounds of film. During the summer of 1992, she embarked on a long-term project on the Navajo reservation in Utah and Arizona. Encompassing landscapes as well as portraits, the project will allow her to use the banquet as well as a more conventional 8 x 10 format.

Her grants and fellowships include an NEA in 1979 and a Guggenheim in 1984. She has enjoyed one-person shows at the New School for Social Research, New York; the Philadelphia College of Art; the Cleveland Museum of Art; the University of Akron, Akron, Ohio; and the Santa Barbara Museum of Art. Her work resides in the permanent collections of the Museum of Modern Art; Metropolitan Museum of Art; San Francisco Museum of Art; Detroit Institute of the Arts; Victoria and Albert Museum; and Yale University Art Gallery.

She lives in New York City and commutes to Yale University where since 1991 she has been an assistant professor, teaching photography in the M.F.A. program.

—Richard B. Woodward

Technical information

Lois Conner owns more than thirty cameras but since 1982 has photographed primarily with a 7 x 17-inch "banquet camera." Of the more than five in her possession, she currently prefers a Folmer Schwing model designed in America. Her main lens is a 14-inch Schneider Krauznach; her backup is a 10 ¾-inch Computar. She uses Kodak film. After testing more than 150 papers, she now prints exclusively on an all-rag Bienfant 360. "This paper, which is designed to be used with felt-tip markers, is by far the best I've ever found." She sensitizes the paper with salts of iron and salts of platinum and palladium. Her contact prints are exposed with an N-1000 mercury vapor lamp.